FAITH THAT WORKS

Applying God's Word to the Job Search

Saskia N. Clay-Rooks

Glenda Sullivan Lee

DEDICATION

This book is dedicated to God, our families, friends, and
job seekers needing encouragement.

CONTENTS

Introduction i

Job search style survey 1

How to use this book 6

Pray 8

Visualize 10

Believe 12

Allocate time 14

Commit 16

Organize 18

Choose wisely 20

Be accountable 22

Assess skills 24

Brand yourself 26

Target employers 28

Engage your network 30

Gather information 32

Determine salary 34

Attend professional conferences 36

Close the gap 38

Become more effective 40

Package your brand 42

Apply 44

Find keywords 46

Customize your cover letter 48

Tailor your résumé 50

Get a witness 52

Uncover hidden opportunities 54

Volunteer 56

Practice interviewing 58

Tell your story 60

Move on 62

Get in position 64

Be flexible 66

Try humility 68

Stand 70

Seek help 72

Rejuvenate 74

Keep going 76

Act anyway 78

No excuses 80

Evaluate the offer 82

Wrap-up right 84

Conclusion 86

Exercises and examples 88

40 Job search tasks 104

**Sample job announcement with tailored résumé and
customized cover letter** 108

About the Authors 119

INTRODUCTION

Searching for a job is an act of faith. It is your hope and trust in the Lord that will sustain you given the uncertainty of the employment market, mitigate your fear of stepping outside of your comfort zone to find new opportunities, and minimize the blow of rejection before being offered a position. That is why *Faith that Works: Applying God's Word to the Job Search* was written---to help Christians going through a job search combine their faith with concrete actions that are proven to increase their chances of successfully securing employment and fulfilling their purpose.

With limitless online job-boards to browse, often conflicting advice on how to write an effective résumé, and general confusion about what networking really means, you might find the job search to be rather daunting. This book is designed to break down the job search into manageable tasks complete with scriptural inspiration, examples, and resources to assist you.

However, simply reading this book will not guarantee that you secure a job. You must read, pray, and act. You must believe in the good things that God has in store for you and the ways that God wants to use you to bless others while vigorously doing your part to engage in the Job Search Tasks. Remember, "faith without works is dead" (James 2:20).

STOP!

Your personality, knowledge about the process involved in finding and applying for positions, and motivation for moving out of your current situation are all factors that could affect your progress. Before going any further, take the quiz in the next section to find out your job search style. An understanding of your beliefs and personal approach to the job search can help you identify what you should keep doing more of, as well as, those things you should begin to incorporate into your strategy even though you have not done them before or they make you feel uneasy.

JOB SEARCH STYLE SURVEY

The following 26-question survey is designed to help you examine your job search style.

- Reflect on all of the positions you have held and roles you have played.

- Consider each statement carefully and then honestly select the number on the scale that best corresponds with your level of agreement or disagreement.

- Do not leave any questions blank.

- If you have not yet experienced a situation, respond based on how you believe you would handle that situation.

0 Strongly Agree   1   2   3   4   5   Strongly Disagree 6

_____1. When asked to talk about my qualifications for a new job, I only mention my previous paid work experience.

_____2. If I heard someone I did not know very well talking about a job opening, I would be reluctant to ask for information.

_____3. If told by employers that they had "no openings," I would be reluctant to ask them to give me the names of other organizations that they think might be hiring at this time.

_____4. I tend to downplay my qualifications and work experience so that an employer does not think that I am too prideful.

_____5. I would rather use an employment agency to find a job than apply to employers directly.

_____6. Before attempting to arrange an interview with an organization, it is not necessary to talk to current employees, take a look at the organization's reports, or check the news for recent developments.

_____7. I hesitate to ask questions when I am being interviewed for a job. I tend to just respond to the questions asked by the interviewer.

_____8. I always apply online. I avoid contacting potential employers by phone or in person.

_____9. I believe a career advisor or mentor would have a better idea of what jobs I should apply for than I do.

_____10. Getting a new job is completely dependent on God, so I do not have to do anything but wait.

_____11. When approaching a company that did not have an advertised position, I would contact Human Resources, rather than the head of the department for which I wanted to work.

_____12. I am reluctant to ask past employers or other people to serve as references or write letters of recommendation for me.

_____13. I think that applying to 3 jobs per week is a lot.

_____14. I do not apply for a job unless I have all of the qualifications listed on the published job description.

_____15. I would not ask an employer for a second interview if I felt the first one went poorly.

_____16. I am reluctant to contact an organization about employment unless I know there is a definite job opening.

_____17. If I did not get a job, I would not contact the organization to ask to be considered for future employment opportunities or other ways to serve them.

_____18. I feel uncomfortable asking friends for job leads.

_____19. With the job market as difficult as it is, I think that I should take whatever job I can get.

_____20. If I felt I was really qualified for the position and someone in Human Resources refused to refer me for an interview, I would give up and not directly contact the head of the Human Resources department or the Hiring Manager to ask them to reconsider my application.

_____21. I am reluctant to contact someone I do not know for information or advice about career opportunities.

_____22. I am devastated when my job application is rejected.

_____23. I have too much time and energy invested in my present job skills. I will not consider changing my occupation.

_____24. After an interview, I usually wait to hear from the interviewer, rather than making contact first to reiterate my interest and summarize my qualifications for the position.

_____25. I spend most of my job search time online instead of connecting with people (e.g., attending conferences, volunteering in the community, taking a class to learn a new job skill).

_____26. I would call an employer when I do not expect him/her to answer the phone, so that I can leave a message instead of speaking with him or her directly.

Transfer your numbered responses from the corresponding questions here and then total each column.

Questions	Questions
1._____	2._____
4._____	3._____
7._____	5._____
9._____	6._____
10._____	8._____
12. _____	11._____
14._____	13._____
16._____	15._____
18._____	17._____
19._____	20._____
21._____	24._____
22._____	25._____
23._____	26._____

Mindset Total: _____   **Engagement Total:**_____

Mark your two scores on the grid below with a dot. Then, connect the dots to determine which quadrant descriptor indicates your current job search style.

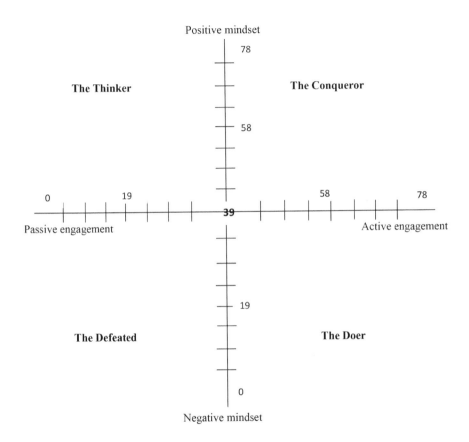

The following section provides recommendations for using this book based on your current job search style.

HOW TO USE THIS BOOK

We recommended that you progress through *Faith that Works* from beginning to end. The Job Search Tasks at the conclusion of each section are designed to build upon one another and move you forward in the job search process. Some actions may take a few hours whereas others can be completed in just ten minutes.

Regardless of your job search style, there are tips to help you capitalize on your strengths and allay your weaknesses.

The Defeated: You have either a negative perception or minimal knowledge of the job search process combined with a passive orientation. Use this book for both inspiration and guidance throughout the various steps of the job search. You are a child of God with special gifts and talents and a powerful call on your life! Renew your mind and actively engage in the Job Search Tasks outlined.

The Thinker: You have difficulty with following through on your well-laid plans. Now take action, particularly in the Job Search Tasks provided in this book that will require you to connect with the people in your network and potential employers. Draw upon your strong sense of who you are and what you can achieve in Christ to step outside of your comfort zone.

The Doer: You have a tendency to act hastily, sometimes without a strategy. There is more power in your thoughts than you think. Be intentional about setting your mind on the positive in order to attract the good outcome that God has planned for you. Make sure to use your dream job or what we will refer to as your visualized job as your reference point when completing the Job Search Tasks.

The Conqueror: Although you are on the right track, there is always room for improvement. Keep on going. Do not grow weary in doing well. There are dozens of Job Search Tasks provided in this book to help maintain your enthusiasm and engagement.

We pray *Faith that Works: Applying God's Word to the Job Search* will provide you with scriptures and Job Search Tasks to keep you inspired to act until you land a new position.

PRAY

"And pray in the Spirit on all occasions with all kinds of prayers and requests." Ephesians 6:18 (NIV)

Unemployment or dissatisfaction with a current position can be a source of suffering and worry. This is precisely why prayer should be a constant from the start to the finish of your job search. Prayer has the power to change things–your situation, your outlook, or perhaps both. Before engaging in job search activities, you should pray for God's favor, wisdom, and direction over the journey on which you are about to embark.

Prayer can be a ready help as you tackle the many choices you will encounter in the job search such as how to allocate your time between different job search strategies, which organizations to target, and what to highlight in your application to gain the favor of the employer. These are all occasions to call upon the Lord for wisdom.

Should you begin to question your abilities or the plan God has for you because you are not getting positions for which you are qualified, then that is the time to build your prayers upon God's Word.

Ask God to renew your mind

with the knowledge that all things are possible through Christ Jesus who strengthens you (Philippians 4:13).   Pray for God to fulfill His promise to supply your every need (Philippians 4:19).

However, after praying you are not to sit idly as you wait for God to deliver your job to you. Instead, wait expectantly. This means to believe, as demonstrated through action, like you have already received whatever you asked for in prayer (Mark 11:24). This could translate to using language like w*hen* I start my new job instead of *if* I ever get a job, maintaining a traditional 8:00 a.m. - 5:00 p.m. workday schedule to complete your job search tasks, and moving to the city where you would like to work before actually securing a job there.

Of course once you accept a job offer, your prayers should turn to praise---thanking God as the source of your blessing.

Your Job Search Task:

Write a job search prayer to recite daily and ask trusted others to pray on your behalf as well.

VISUALIZE

"If it is serving, let him serve; if it teaching let him teach; if it is encouraging, let him encourage; if it is contributing to the needs of others, let him give generously; if it is leadership, let him govern diligently; if it is showing mercy, let him do it cheerfully." Romans 12:7-8 (NIV)

When looking for a job, your first instinct may be to find a position like the one you previously held or the one your parents, spouse, or friends have told you to pursue. Instead, ask God to help you visualize the ideal role for you.

Consider your likes and dislikes

and what interests and excites you. Picture exactly what you enjoy doing at work. What skills and talents are you using? Are you working in an office, outside, or traveling most of the time? Are you primarily interacting with people, data, or tools? With whom are you working? Is the culture highly structured and policy-oriented or one that thrives on creativity and flexibility?

The visualization exercise is one you may need to do a few times in order to have certainty about the components of your ideal role. It is also okay if you do not initially have a name or job title for your vision. Simply being able to describe the components of your best fit role is a good start and will be helpful when conducting Internet and in-person research. It will also allow you to provide an answer to the question your friends will undoubtedly ask, "What do you want to do?" Remember to use the visualization information in evaluating the job offers that you will receive. While every aspect of your visualized job may not be present in a real job opportunity, it will be constructive in helping you decide whether to accept or decline it.

Keep in mind, God wants us to enjoy all aspects of our lives. God does not want us to dread going to work. God wants our occupations to be another way for us to express the gifts He has given us. When we work in our talent areas, we are happy and our joy can draw others to us and thereby aid us in carrying out the instructions Jesus provided in the Great Commission (Matthew 28:19) - to bring more disciples to Christ.

Your Job Search Task:

Complete the visualization exercise on page 88 to create an ideal job description.

BELIEVE

"With the tongue we praise our Lord and Father, and with it can curse men, who have been made in God's likeness. Out of the same mouth come praise and cursing. My brothers, this should not be." James 3:9-10 (NIV)

Children often believe the saying "Sticks and stones may break your bones but words can never hurt you." As adults we know that the temporary pain associated with a broken arm pales in comparison to the deep damage harmful thoughts and words can cause a person. Are any of the following job search beliefs playing on repeat in your mind? "The economy is terrible and I'll never find a good job," "There's no way someone like me will ever get hired," or "When I hit send, my résumé just goes into a black hole, so why should I bother?" If so, this kind of

Negative self-talk does not line up with the promises God has spoken about your life

and you need to stop it now. This is what Satan wants you to believe. Satan is using your pessimistic thoughts and words in an attempt to draw you away from God's plan for your life. Do not let him succeed. God has made it clear that in our lives we will have good times and bad. In all situations He expects his children to stand firm in His promises in thought, word, and deed.

God has fulfilled His promises in so many situations when man said "no way." God blessed Abraham and Sarah with a son in their old age, He parted the Red Sea to free the Israelites from slavery, and raised Jesus from the dead. These are only a few examples to remind you to believe in God's promises to you. Matthew 6:26 tells us that God takes care of the fowls in the air and that we are much more valuable to the Father than they are. Create a new and positive playlist for your mind: "Yes, the economy may be bad and God will take care of me," "God will make a way for me to be hired," and "Job searching is hard, yet God will make sure the right people know of my talents and will review my application materials."

Your responsibility while looking for a job is to exhibit behavior that will serve as a testament to others that you are child of God. Therefore, make the decision to believe what God said He will do for you. Choose to stop every self-defeating thought and exchange it with one that demonstrates to you and others that you agree with God about what He has planned for your life.

Your Job Search Task:

Replace all negative self-talk statements with positive ones.

ALLOCATE TIME

"For everything there is a season, and a time for every matter under heaven...a time to plant, and a time to pluck up what is planted" Ecclesiastes 3:1-2 (RSV)

With every application you submit, you will be planting another seed. How long until harvest time? A rule of thumb is to expect your job search to last one month for every $10,000 you seek in gross salary. Therefore, if your preferred salary is $60,000 per year, you could reasonably anticipate six months or more to get your dream or visualized job. God works in His own time to provide us with our desires and expects us to be productive while eagerly awaiting the great things He has in store for us. What does "productive" look like? It means continuing to pursue your ideal job (visualized job) while at the same time securing additional ways (pay the bills jobs) to meet your financial or other needs.

Here is a timeline to help you figure out how to allocate your job search time:

Months 0-2: Allocate 90% of time/energy to Visualized job; 10% to Pay the bills job

Months 3-4: Allocate 70% of time/energy to Visualized job; 30% to Pay the bills job

Months 5-6: Allocate 50% of time/energy to Visualized job; 50% to Pay the bills job

Months 6+ : Allocate 30% of time/energy to Visualized job; 70% to Pay the bills job

Believe your "visualized job" prayer will
be answered in God's timing

and your faithfulness will be rewarded more abundantly than you can imagine.

Your Job Search Task:

Using the guidelines provided, mark on your calendar the amount of time each month you will allocate to both your visualized and pay the bills job searches.

COMMIT

"If a man vows a vow to the Lord, or swears an oath to bind himself by a pledge, he shall not break his word. He shall do according to all that proceeds out of his mouth."
Numbers 30:2 (RSV)

God has given us time and the choice of how we will use it. If you are not employed, allot 36 hours or more per week to engage in job search activities. If you are employed, then set aside at least 12 hours per week. You may be thinking, 12 hours? I don't have it. My schedule is so full now. In order to change your employment situation, you must conduct an honest and close examination of how you spend your time. What are some of your regular activities? Can you begin to say "no" to things such as watching television or playing video games in order to schedule time for your job search? Intentionally committing time to your job search will result in you knowing that you are giving 100% to your goal.

Once you have dedicated the recommended amount of hours, look at your calendar and schedule job search appointments six days per week. (You too get one day of rest). These time blocks are critical and should be treated like other important tasks that you make time for daily such as housekeeping, helping your children with their homework, or preparing dinner. Be mindful that if you cancel your appointment and say "yes" to a non-job search activity during your scheduled job search time, you are not making finding a new job a priority.

Strive not to be an "all or nothing" doer in your job search.

Believe in the power and potential results of "a little bit." This means that if on a scheduled two-hour job search day, you find yourself with only 20 minutes due to an unexpected issue that requires immediate attention, do something during those 20 minutes instead of doing nothing at all and make up the difference at a later date.

Your Job Search Task:

Schedule job search appointments on your calendar and vow to keep the meetings.

ORGANIZE

"But everything should be done in a fitting and orderly way."
1 Corinthians 14:40 (NIV)

Step one in the job search is to set up your space, resources, and process. It is certain that there are numerous factors in the job search which are out of your control and therefore it is essential that you

Take control in all areas that you can

Being organized can provide a much needed sense of comfort in an otherwise hectic situation.

- Designate a location to serve as your work space to find your next workplace. Pray that this space is one you enter with an open-mind, focus, and drive.

- Utilize a spreadsheet or a job search binder to record your "To Do" list, target employer names and acquired research data, networking contacts, informational interview insights, and job interview notes.

- Maintain one calendar to post all of your appointments, dates to follow-up on applications, commitments to anyone who suggested you call them in a few weeks, and the schedule of what you will do daily or weekly.

- Create an "Applications Submitted" folder to keep descriptions of all the jobs you have applied to, as well as, copies of the résumé/cover letter and/ or application form sent. Many employers will remove position descriptions from their website and other job boards after the application deadline has passed. If you are selected for an interview, having this information will greatly assist in your preparation.

- Make a "Potential Jobs" folder. Here is where you will keep any leads such as newspaper stories, Chamber of Commerce updates, or ideas you have on how to add value to prospective employers or clients.

Your Job Search Task:

Determine your job search space and set up an organized process to help you stay on track.

CHOOSE WISELY

"Iron sharpens iron, and one man sharpens another."
Proverbs 27:17 (ESV)

Be careful who you tell about your desires for a promotion, that you are open to moving away to take the right job, or that you have just received another rejection. If you do not choose your confidants wisely, instead of support, encouragement, and a confidence boost, you may receive jealousy, discouragement, and an "I told you so." Depending on their personality, where they are in their Christian experience, or the circumstances they are currently dealing with, even your closest family and friends may not be able to be good companions to you during your job search journey.

Throughout the employment hunt, you will travel across hills, valleys, and forests where you will undoubtedly experience moments of frustration, confusion, and exhaustion. Therefore it is of paramount importance that you do your best to

Avoid toxic people

along the way. These negative individuals can quickly be identified by the following three characteristics: 1) When you are down and feeling sorry for yourself, they not only join, but become the life of your pity party; 2) When you are feeling timid about taking a leap of faith that would expand your horizons, instead of pushing you, they hold you back by planting seeds of guilt and fear of failure; 3) When you are encouraged by a small success, they steal your joy with demeaning words and a bleak outlook.

Do not let yourself be destroyed by fools. Invite men and women with wisdom to walk alongside of you. We recommend that you choose positive, faithful people to accompany you. An obvious choice might be someone who knows you professionally, like a colleague or mentor in the field. Alternatively, you may choose to consider someone who can be completely objective, such as a career counselor or life coach. Perhaps you would be well-served to sojourn with fellow job seekers by joining a job club that offers accountability, resource sharing, and networking potential.

Your Job Search Task:

Pray that God steers you away from harmful people and places healthy, life-affirming guides along your path exactly where and when you need them most.

BE ACCOUNTABLE

"Two are better than one, because they have a good return for their work." Ecclesiastes 4:9 (NIV)

Searching for a job most likely ranks with getting a root canal and public speaking as one of the most dreaded things to do. If you are looking for work because you have been laid off, you may feel embarrassment or shame. If you are currently employed in a role that is not the right fit due to a bad boss or wrong work culture, it is understandable that you do not want to broadcast your desire to find a new place of employment. Regardless of your particular situation, it is a mistake to look for new work in isolation.

This is definitely a time when you need to reach out and ask for help. For you, asking for assistance may be a foreign concept. As a Christian, you may be more accustomed to being in the role of giving aid, rather than receiving it. Right now, you are probably thinking of all the reasons why you will not seek help. Be careful that pride is not responsible for your excuses. Prideful thinking and actions are not pleasing to God. God intentionally places us in positions of need to remind us that nothing we receive is due to our efforts alone.

Looking for a job is an opportunity God is giving you to strengthen the bonds with those in your life, a way to widen your connections to meet new people, and yes, also to find out how you can potentially benefit those who are assisting you. We all have heard of the saying "two heads are better than one." That principle applies in your job search as you should enlist the support of an accountability partner.

What is an accountability partner? This is a person to whom you will

Make commitments regarding your job search activities

and check in with weekly. Your accountability partner will be the person with whom you share your successes and frustrations. He or she will be your personal cheerleader and drill sergeant when needed. Your accountability partner is someone with whom you will discuss job search strategies and who will provide you with wise counsel when evaluating opportunities. Pray to God for direction regarding the individuals you should consider. You need someone who will be honest and not agree with you simply to make you feel better. As to not strain your relationship, our recommendation is that you select someone other than your spouse or significant other to serve in this critical role.

Your Job Search Task:

Ask someone to be your accountability partner.

ASSESS SKILLS

"Therefore, if anyone is in Christ, he is a new creation; the old has gone, the new has come."
2 Corinthians 5:17 (NIV)

Since completing the visualization exercise (pages 10 and 88), you have some idea of what your ideal role is. The next step is to

Take a look at all you know how to do,

or what is commonly referred to as your skill set. From a career perspective, skills are often categorized as transferable, job-specific, and self-management.

Transferable skills are valued by most employers, regardless of industry, and thus can easily be applied in various job roles. Common transferable skills are researching, problem solving, writing, analyzing data, managing projects, organizing, communicating, and team-building.

Job-specific skills refer to particular knowledge that is required for a certain occupation. For instance, human resource compensation specialists must know how to classify jobs and understand pension plans. Lawyers are required to counsel clients about their legal rights and recommend courses of action.

Self-management skills, also known as work traits, demonstrate your ability to perform well in a professional environment. These skills include attention to detail, punctuality, open-mindedness, and being a calculated risk-taker to name a few.

To assist you in generating a relevant list of skills for your career interests, go to the Internet and search websites which specialize in the types of jobs you are seeking. For example, if you are a non-profit manager, you most certainly will want to bookmark Idealist.org. Once at your choice job board, read 10-20 postings for positions that interest you. Location and type of employer are not important for this activity. Simply compile a list of the most common transferable, job, and self-management skills that are qualifications for the positions you find attractive.

Then, on this same list, place a check next to all the skills you possess. In doing so, reflect upon the various paid and unpaid, academic, and non-academic experiences you have had and identify the skills used. This is not the time to be shy and under-rate yourself. Completion of the process is important as it is an exercise to help you gain more appreciation for the diverse skill set you have to offer employers.

Your Job Search Task:

Complete a skill assessment as explained above.

BRAND YOURSELF

"Then the LORD came down in the cloud and stood there with him and proclaimed his name, the LORD. And he passed in front of Moses, proclaiming, "The LORD, the LORD, the compassionate and gracious God, slow to anger, abounding in love and faithfulness, maintaining love to thousands, and forgiving wickedness, rebellion and sin."
Exodus 34:5-7 (NIV)

Throughout the Bible, verses like Exodus 34 describe what God is like. There are also other passages that show what God is not like. This is often done by positioning God in contrast to humans such as in Numbers 23:19 which reads, "God is not a man, that he should lie, nor a son of man, that he should change his mind." Whether from what you have read, heard in sermons or experienced from a personal relationship with God, the name LORD has meaning. Perhaps, you, like many people, would use the words loving, giving, merciful, jealous, patient, ever-present, distant, or incomprehensible to express the nature of the LORD. These images, feelings, and expectations that are conjured up can, in a way, be seen as the LORD's brand.

Simply put, a brand is one's perceived value relative to others. What brand would you like to have associated with your name? What is at the core of who you are as a being? What knowledge, skills, and abilities do you possess? How do you stand out compared to the competition? It is imperative for you as a job seeker to know who you are, what you want to do, and how you can

Add unique value to an organization.

Here are a few things you can do to identify your brand: 1) Think about the kinds of projects for which your expertise is consistently sought; 2) Ask your friends, family, colleagues, supervisors, and clients what your strengths are; and 3) Consider taking an assessment such as the Myers Briggs Type Indicator which can be administered and interpreted by a career counselor.

If you are a career changer or come to discover that how you see yourself is not how others see you, then you will need to take proactive steps to build a new brand. This can be achieved through developing a skill, updating your wardrobe so that you also look the part of a professional in your field of choice, and deliberately talking about your passion with those around you. In fact, you should package your brand in a clear and concise statement that can be easily incorporated into your introduction when meeting new people, cover letters, and responses to common interview questions.

Your Job Search Task:

Write a 1-2 sentence brand statement that tells what you are best at and who you serve (e.g., I energize, focus, and align manufacturing organizations resulting in sustainable acceleration of processes, reduction in waste, and growth in profits).

TARGET EMPLOYERS

"But in your hearts set apart Christ as Lord. Always be prepared to give an answer to everyone who asks you to give the reason for the hope that you have." 1 Peter 3:15 (NIV)

As Christians, our Lord expects us to always be ready to answer questions about our faith and why we choose to serve Him. As a job seeker, you can expect the question "what employer do you want to work for?" You should be prepared to provide the names of several potential companies and why you are interested in them. Earlier you visualized your ideal job, now it is time to develop a list of employers who need workers to do what you are interested in doing. How many organizations should be on your list? Ideally 25-100. At this stage in your job search, you are trying to

Create opportunities not close them off.

Your list of potential employers should include *all* of the organizations in your target geographic location that hire people with your qualifications and interests. Where do you begin? Start with major employers that you already know about through your network. Then, move on to these resources to identify others:

    *Department of Commerce for your target state

    *Chamber of Commerce website for your target city/county

    *LinkedIn profiles of people with your desired job titles

*Relevant professional association membership lists

*Industry journals (e.g., *Washington Business Journal*)

*Local or university library for company guides such as *Hoover's* and *Vault*

It can be challenging to actively pursue say 50 organizations at a time, therefore, we recommend you rank order your list so that your most desired employers are in your top 10. Review each employer's website and social media platforms and use factors such as their mission, impact in the community, and reputation to determine their placement on your list. Keep in mind, employer rankings are dynamic and could change based on any updated information you gather.

Your Job Search Task:

Create a ranked list of at least 25 potential employers.

ENGAGE YOUR NETWORK

*"When they saw the courage of Peter and John and realized
that they were unschooled, ordinary men, they were astonished
and they took note that these men had been with Jesus."*
Acts 4:13 (NIV)

In the book of Acts we learn how God used Peter and John to perform the miraculous healing of a man who had been lame from birth. Soon after the news spread, the two disciples were captured, jailed, and brought before the high priest and his court for an interrogation. The rulers, elders, and teachers of the law were astounded that these mere fishermen could yield such healing power.

As a job seeker, you have hopefully planned to tap into the networking potential of the alumni association at each of the schools you have attended, your sorority or fraternity, and any professional organizations to which you belong. These are great groups to start with as they often maintain a searchable database of individuals willing to be contacted by people looking for career advice and mentorship. However, do not stop there!

Have you thought to

Update *everyone* in your network about
your current career interests?

When catching up with your neighbor, fitness coach, dentist, or son's Boy Scout leader, have you mentioned the kind of job opportunity you are looking for? If not, ask yourself why not? Is it that you have made assumptions based on someone's age, background, employment status, or title as to whether or not they might have information, advice, or contacts that could be useful? Beware of an elitist mindset like that of the leaders illustrated in the scripture. Start making a list of *everyone* (barring any toxic individuals) you know from all the facets of your life including: family, friends, church, previous jobs, and volunteer organizations.

As you write down each person's name, remember that he or she will likely have a list just as long, or longer than yours. If one of your immediate contacts does not know of a job, he or she may know of someone who does! Do not be surprised if God chooses to use an unlikely agent to bless you in your job search.

Your Job Search Task:

Complete the "My Network Diagram" on page 90.

GATHER INFORMATION

"Ask and it will be given to you; seek and you will find;
knock and the door will be opened to you. For everyone who
asks receives; he who seeks finds; and to him who knocks the
door will be opened." Matthew 7:7-8 (NIV)

What barber gives the cleanest shave? Which church has the most inspirational preacher? Who is the best mechanic in town? Where can you get the juiciest burgers? These are the kinds of questions most of us will easily ask several friends, casual acquaintances, and even strangers. Use this same willingness to seek answers in gathering important data for your job search. There is actually a name for this data collecting process---informational interviewing. Why this approach? Because you should first gather information to determine whether or not an employer is a good fit and you are truly interested in working there. Asking open-ended questions instead of "Are you hiring right now?" may lead to knowledge of pending opportunities within that company, as well as, referrals to hiring managers at other employers on your target list.

An informational interview is a career conversation you initiate with people working in the roles, organizations, and professions that are of interest to you for the purpose of gathering information and advice. Most people enjoy helping job seekers by sharing their insights based on experience. These meetings will allow you to

Get first-hand facts

regarding the ideal job you have visualized. As the person requesting the meeting, you will be responsible for setting the agenda and taking the lead on asking questions. Careful research will generate strategic and thoughtful questions and help you make a positive impression. On page 90 you will find a list of questions you could also ask during an informational interview. Remember, you *cannot*, however, ask for a job at this time. Why? You must stay true to your stated goal. Also, this meeting is not meant to be one-sided. Through your questions and observations look for ways you might be of help to the person you are meeting with and how you might fill the needs of their organization. Propose ideas for a mutually beneficial arrangement in follow-up communications with your contact.

Informational interviews can take place at the advice giver's office, a coffee shop, by phone, or through Skype. How do you find people with whom to request informational interviews? Take a look at the networking diagram you created (see pages 30 and 90). Give each person in your network a brief description of the type of people you are interested in meeting with and ask if they know of someone to whom they can refer you.

Your Job Search Task:

Send out 3 informational interview requests this week. See pages 94-95 for an example.

DETERMINE SALARY

"Give us each day, our daily bread." Luke 11:3 (NIV)

Salary history, salary required, and salary desired---you must be prepared to communicate all of this information at any point in your job search. It might be requested on an application, during a phone screening, or at an interview. Although salary history may appear as the easiest to share, it is in actuality more complicated than just what your take-home pay has been during your years of professional employment. First, it is vital to provide your gross pay and not your net pay. Additionally, it is important to factor in your benefits, which depending on your former employers, could represent a significant percentage of your total compensation (e.g., medical benefits, retirement plan contributions). Why are you being asked to provide this historical information? Most often because salary is a fast way to screen out applicants. If your number is too low, you will be considered as inexperienced or desperate. If your number is too high, you may be quickly dismissed as overqualified or unaffordable.

So what is the best strategy? Before you apply to any opportunity, it is imperative that you

Conduct research through informational interviews and Internet sources

to get a sense of the current market rate for the types of roles you are seeking. Also, remember to factor in the cost of living for all geographic locations you are considering. Once you have your data, know that you do not have to reveal your hand first – even if the question is being asked during an interview. When the interviewer presents the salary question, politely ask them "what salary range has been budgeted for this position?" If they give you the range, you can consider that information in determining your answer. If they do not give you the budgeted number, you have not lost anything as you were ready with your prepared response. In either case, add that the number you give them is flexible which may allow you to remain in consideration.

In regard to salary required, spend time putting pen to paper or mouse to spreadsheet to specifically determine the annual salary requirements needed to meet your living expenses, savings, and debts. However, is a salary increase desired as one of your expected new job outcomes? Research is again required to find out if your situation has the likelihood of providing more money. For example, if you are currently employed in the non-profit sector and change to private industry doing similar work, then odds are favorable that you could be offered a higher salary. However, moving in the opposite direction, from a for-profit organization to a non-profit one, your starting salary may be less. Another factor which could reduce your take home pay is changing careers, say from an academic reference librarian (master's degree required) to an elementary school teacher (bachelor's degree required). While the hiring manager may subjectively appreciate your advanced degree, additional years of experience, or other extras you bring to the table, they objectively can point out that the add-ons are not needed for the job and therefore will not modify their salary budget to accommodate your desired salary.

Your Job Search Task:

Conduct research to collect data on average salaries for your professions of interest based on education, work experience, or other credentials valuable to the marketplace.

ATTEND PROFESSIONAL CONFERENCES

"He who walks with the wise grows wise."
Proverbs 13:4 (NIV)

The Bible tells us that wisdom is supreme. Where should you go to get wise about your career options and possible job opportunities? Conferences, symposia, and meetings. We are not meant to function in isolation, but rather in relationship with others as part of a larger body that includes more seasoned individuals with good advice for us. Professional organizations provide occasions to gather for the purposes of sharing best practices, discussing the main challenges, and charting the future course of a particular field. These events are among the best places to identify and meet the major players in an industry from across the country or the globe, see demonstrations of the newest technologies, and learn about business ventures.

If you are not currently a member of a professional group, join one today as this will reduce your conference registration fee and come with many other benefits. To find out which organization you should become a member of, ask your colleagues for recommendations, search on LinkedIn for events, or do web research through the Internet Public Library resource (www.ipl.org). There is a group for every profession including the: American Association of School Administrators, Academy for Health Services Research and Health Policy, Society for Computational Economics, and American Advertising Federation. Many national organizations break down into smaller chapters by region or state. Becoming a member and attending conferences at the local level is more economical and can provide a more intimate atmosphere for you to network. After all, the primary purpose of going to a conference is not to win a door prize, but rather for you to "confer" or talk with and

Gain understanding from as many professionals, thought leaders, and hiring managers as you can.

Go with a strategy. Plan to stay very close to the meeting site and take advantage of all of the activities and sessions, as well as, the meals and social outings for the entire conference. Look over the list of attendees to identify individuals who work at your target organizations that you will try to meet. Prepare and practice how you will introduce yourself. Develop questions to ask as a way to learn more about the skills most valued in the job market, the types of projects that are in the works, and where the greatest hiring needs are. Do not forget to exchange business cards so that you can later follow-up with everyone you encounter.

Your Job Search Task:

Identify and register for a professional meeting or conference.

CLOSE THE GAP

"Forget the former things; do not dwell on the past. See, I am doing a new thing."
Isaiah 43:18-19 (NIV)

Most new things are looked upon positively and with anticipation --- new baby, new house, and yes, a new job. Yet, the changes that come with a new phase in life can also bring on feelings of insecurity, anxiety, and fear. After reviewing job postings and conducting informational interviews with numerous career subject matter experts, you may have learned that you need fresh skills in order to meet the job requirements employers are seeking. Do not let this discourage you. In order for God to take you to the next level,

Approach the need to acquire new skills with optimism and faith.

How can you gain skills to close the gap between where you are and where you want to be? Search for reputable training programs that offer seminars on the topic. Community colleges may have semester-long courses or brief continuing education classes. For hands on training, contact non-profit organizations including your church to find out if you could volunteer several hours a week to build proficiency and contribute to their mission. Look over your contact list to determine if someone in your network is experienced in the skill and work out an arrangement for them to teach you what you need in exchange for a good or service you can provide. Finally, depending on the skill needed, consider teaching yourself. There are a number of "how to" tutorials online and in books you can get from the public library.

Your Job Search Task:

Gain or strengthen the required skills for your new job.

BECOME MORE EFFECTIVE

"Do you not know that in a race all the runners run, but only one gets the prize? Run in such a way as to get the prize." 1 Corinthians 9:24 (NIV)

There are several ways to find out about job openings and become a candidate, but different job search and application methods do not all yield equal results. Some are much more effective than others. It is widely held that up to 80% of jobs are filled by word of mouth, also known as networking. Have you ever wondered how this can be true?

Put yourself in the shoes of a small company manager. You have a major deliverable due to a client in three months and one of your best employees has just given you his two week notice.

Unfortunately, since he possesses a skill-set that nobody else on staff has, you must get his position filled as soon as possible. What will you do? Sign-up to recruit at the next local career fair? Nope, the registration fee is too high. Advertise the vacancy on Craig's List? Better not, the last time you were completely overwhelmed with the volume of applications you received for a single position. Plus, due to the sensitive nature of the project and high expectations of the client, you need someone you can trust. You remember the woman you met with about two months ago at her request. She presented herself very well, asked insightful questions about your current projects and followed-up appropriately with a thank you note and copy of her résumé. You place the call, and to your delight she is available to come in for an interview the following week.

All runners in the job search race can point and click behind the comforting anonymity of a computer screen, which makes the competition for jobs advertised online extremely keen. What will move you closer to your goal is to

Strategically build relationships with decision makers at your target organizations

through informational interviewing. This way, you will be the first person who comes to mind when they have or are asked to refer someone for a position. If you want to win the prize of that job offer, you should prioritize networking as a job search strategy.

Your Job Search Task:

Send out 3 more informational interview requests this week. See pages 94-95 for an example.

PACKAGE YOUR BRAND

*"Conduct yourselves with wisdom toward outsiders, making
the most of the opportunity. Let your speech always be with
grace, as though seasoned with salt."*
Colossians 4:5-6 (NASB)

People are listening and watching you at all times. Given your identity as a Christian, teacher, scientific writer, or experienced accountant others will have certain expectations of you. They will be looking for congruency between what you say and what you do, between your public and private image.

Doing a Google search on candidates is becoming standard practice for hiring managers. Whereas having a negative presence is clearly detrimental to your chances for employment, not having any web presence at all can be nearly as damaging because an employer or prospective customer may have less information about you and your work than for your competitors. Delete any unflattering pictures from Facebook and replace them with pictures from the conference you just attended. Instead of updating the world about what you are cooking for dinner, have your status reflect that you are doing pro bono work today. Complete a profile, ask for recommendations from colleagues, and join relevant groups on the professional networking site LinkedIn. Also, get on Twitter. It is a great venue for demonstrating that you are on top of current issues in your field. Share or "retweet" news articles, comment on hot topics and "follow" major players and organizations in your industry. Finally, if you haven't already, consider blogging or creating a personal webpage. They are great spaces to showcase your writing skills, exhibit your portfolio, and

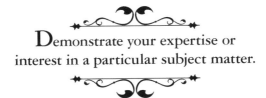

Demonstrate your expertise or interest in a particular subject matter.

To ensure that you are not confused with anyone else, package your brand across all platforms —cover letter, résumé, business cards, the three major social media outlets, your website, in person, etc. Say and write your name exactly the same way everywhere and use matching font type and style where applicable. Display the identical profile picture of yourself on Facebook, LinkedIn, and Twitter. Include your webpage or LinkedIn profile URL on the bottom of your email signature block and on your business card.

As a Christian, have your fellow church members witnessed you respond to bad news with calmness and hope? Teachers, have you demonstrated your ability to engage young people in lessons using the newest technology? If a scientific writer, do you communicate complicated scientific advancements in lay people terms? All the accountants, have you led by example by keeping your personal finances in order? Remember, branding is show and tell.

Your Job Search Task:

Create a LinkedIn profile, give yourself a Facebook Facelift or start following target organizations on Twitter as a way to build and spread your brand.

APPLY

"She looks for wool and flax, And works with her hands in delight. She is like merchant ships; She brings her food from afar. She rises also while it is still night. And gives food to her household, And portions to her maidens. She considers a field and buys it; From her earnings she plants a vineyard." Proverbs 31: 13-16 (NASB)

As a job seeker, what does "to apply" mean to you? To find a job announcement online, upload a résumé and hit send? Sure. That is definitely one reading of the word apply---to submit credentials for employment. However, consider for a moment this definition of apply---to

Devote oneself or one's efforts to something fully.

How much more fruitful could your job search be if you gave it your all? The woman in the text can teach us a great deal about being completely committed to becoming successful.

Be resourceful. She had help. Enlist your network to aide you in your job search. Ask around to see if anyone you know has connections at your target employers. Perhaps, they could refer you to someone within the organizations for more information that would be useful in finding hidden opportunities or putting together a great application. In addition, you would then have insiders who could put in a good word for you or ensure that your application received serious consideration. *Be industrious.* The Bible character got up while it was still dark. Put in the extra time to develop customized application materials for each job that you apply to. In your cover letter, demonstrate your understanding of the organization based on the research you have done on their website, by following the news, and talking to people. Send a cover letter even if it is not required. *Be versatile.* The woman of Proverbs 31 was not just a farmer, but a seamstress and merchant as well. She did not rely on just one method of providing for her family. Do not limit yourself to a single way of applying for jobs. Use several different methods to try to get your knowledge, skills, and abilities noticed by people who have the power to hire you. After submitting your application via email, follow-up with a paper copy mailed to the hiring manager to double your exposure. This would also cover you in case your application went into the spam mail folder or your attachment could not be opened. Then, two weeks after the application deadline, follow-up with a phone call to express your continued interest in the position, reiterate your qualifications, and ask for an interview.

Your Job Search Task:

Apply to a job.

FIND KEYWORDS

"So shall my word be that goes out from my mouth; it shall not return to me empty, but it shall accomplish that which I purpose, and succeed in the thing for which I sent it."
Isaiah 55:11 (NSRV)

Given that organizations may receive hundreds of applications for a single position, one purpose of the Human Resources department is to whittle down the pile of applicants to a manageable number for the hiring official. Therefore, it is crucial for job seekers to get the attention of recruiters, hiring managers, and anyone who is selecting candidates for job interviews. The best way of doing that is to speak their language. Keywords are usually descriptors which indicate skills, work qualities, and experiences that signal to the application reviewer that you understand what they do and have what it takes to solve their staffing need.

Although you may spend hours preparing your applications materials, employers generally spend less than 30 seconds determining who they will consider for employment and who they will not. In small organizations, it is likely the reviewer will be a person and in larger ones, it is highly probable the preliminary decision-maker will be a computer. The computer program will take nanoseconds skimming your résumé searching for the right words. Failure to include these keywords is almost a guarantee of rejection. Where do you find keywords? Read several job postings to

Determine what qualifications and duties are commonly mentioned for the positions you are seeking.

Review your informational interview notes for recurring experiences and traits of successful professionals in your chosen occupation. For instance, keywords for the marketing field could include market research, focus groups, forecast, revenue increases, promotion strategy, strategic sales, trade show management, and media planning.

Make a list of the keywords for your target positions and then think of times when you have used these highly sought-after qualifications to contribute to an employer or organization. If you want your job search materials to accomplish the purpose of getting you noticed, then you must use keywords and provide illustrations to back up your claims that you have what it takes to get the job done. Your keyword examples must be included in all written and verbal job search communications---emails, cover letters, résumés, LinkedIn profile, networking conversations, interviews, blog postings, etc.

Your Job Search Task:

Research and make a list of attention-getting and important keywords for the job roles you are currently seeking.

CUSTOMIZE YOUR COVER LETTER

*"Do not work for your own good. Think of what you can do for others."*1 Corinthians 10:24 (NLV)

What is the purpose of the cover letter? To answer why. More specifically, to explain why you are applying to *this* job at *this* organization. There are many valid reasons why you would be applying to any given job. "I need the money." "I think this job would help me build the skills that I need for the job I really want." "I want to work for a big name company like this one because of the doors it will open for me." Be careful that you do not fall into the trap of making the cover letter all about what your interests are and what you can get out of the experience.

An easy way to tell if you have fallen prey to self-centeredness while writing a cover letter is if the majority of your sentences begin with the word "I." In order to resist the temptation to make the cover letter all about you rephrase the "why" question like this. Why are you the best person to fill the employer's needs? In other words, how would hiring you be good for them? For this you will need to reference the position description or reflect on a previous informational interview. For each requirement, identify concrete examples which show how you are qualified to meet that need. Refer to your skill assessment (see page 24) and select your strongest illustrations to include in your one-page cover letter. Whenever possible,

Incorporate keywords from the announcement or
conversation you have had with an insider.

Make it easy for the employer to see what a great fit you are for the position
by explicitly stating how your previous experiences have prepared you to fulfill the
expectations of the role. Also, in your letter attempt to reference information you
found on the organization's website or a recent news article you read about their
major upcoming contract or an award they won. Finally, review the online staff
directory, ask a personal contact within the organization, or call to find out the
name and title of the person to whom you should be addressing your letter.

Customizing your cover letter in this way for each position, as well as, sending
a cover letter even when it is not requested will make the employer feel that you
are genuinely interested in their organization and the work they do. The best cover
letters are those that are employer-focused and not self-focused. Remember, it is
not about you; it is about them [the employer].

Your Job Search Task:

Write a cover letter tailored to a specific employer/opportunity. For help see page
90 and the sample cover letter on page 117.

TAILOR YOUR RÉSUMÉ

"for by your words you will be justified, and by your words
you will be condemned."
Matthew 12:37 (ESV)

In writing your résumé, your word choices matter. Using the right words correctly could mean the difference between getting an invitation to interview or not. Applicants who submit résumés with typos, misspellings, or grammatical errors are often cut immediately. It is advantageous to arrange the content of your résumé so that your most relevant experience appears as close to the top of your résumé as possible. To ensure that the reader can get a sense of your qualifications at a glance, avoid using generic category headings such as Work Experience and Volunteer Experience. Instead, replace them with more meaningful labels, based on the qualifications for the position, such as Project Management Experience, International Experience or Communications Experience.

Next to go are the applicants who do not use keywords from the position description. It is imperative that you include on your résumé some of the exact words from the job announcement to which you are responding. List required certifications, professional skills, and proficiency in computer programs and languages with qualifiers such as basic, intermediate, advanced, or fluent. Begin your descriptions with strong action-verbs which demonstrate that you have or can perform the responsibilities of the role you are seeking.

Although qualified, the final candidates to get removed from consideration are those who do not stand out. Wherever possible, use numerals, dollar signs, and percentages to quantify your contribution to previous organizations. If you were the first to chair an event, the only consultant assigned to a contract worth $1million or the "Best Staff Member of the Year," say so. Your résumé is not the place to be timid or modest about how God has used you to make a difference. When writing a résumé, incorporate the words that

Justify why the employer should hire you

for the specific job at hand.

Your Job Search Task:

After reviewing the resources on pages 108-116, write a résumé tailored specifically in response to a job announcement.

GET A WITNESS

"I hope in the Lord Jesus to send Timothy to you soon, that I also may be cheered when I receive news about you. I have no one else like him, who will show genuine concern for your welfare. For everyone looks out for their own interests, not those of Jesus Christ. But you know that Timothy has proved himself, because as a son with his father he has served with me in the work of the gospel." Philippians 2:19-22 (NIV)

Hiring new employees is risky business. Organizations invest a substantial amount of financial and human resources into recruiting, interviewing, relocating, and training new staff members without any real guarantee that the relationship will be successful. Will the new hire perform at a satisfactory level? Will her core values match those of the organization? Will he get along with the rest of the team? Employers attempt to mitigate the danger inherent in hiring new employees by conducting background checks and Internet searches, and calling references before making employment offers. Reference checks and letters of recommendation were just as common in Biblical times as today. Hopefully, you

Have people that can speak as highly of you
as Paul did of Timothy

in this scripture.

Unless otherwise specified, when asked to provide references you should list, on a page separate from your résumé, 3-5 people who have witnessed you at your best in a professional capacity. Your reference sheet should always include at least one manager, current or previous. Additionally, mentors, advisors, supervisees, or colleagues are acceptable. Besides the names of your guarantors, indicate their title, place of employment, phone number, email address, and relationship to you. However before you list anyone, you should first get their permission. Schedule a time to update your potential supporters about your current career goals and the status of your job search. After describing the duties and qualifications for the types of positions that you are seeking, ask if they would feel comfortable endorsing you.

It is good practice to alert your references whenever you make it to an on-site interview as it is generally after this point that they would be contacted. In preparation for the call or electronic survey they will receive, make sure to provide your references with the latest version of your résumé, the position description, and talking points on the skills, personal qualities, or accomplishments you hope they will mention. As a professional courtesy, keep your advocates abreast of the progress of your job search. Of course, they should be among the very first people you thank once you have been offered a position!

Your Job Search Task:

Review the sample of a reference page on page 99. Arrange a meeting with your references to update them about your job search.

UNCOVER HIDDEN
OPPORTUNITIES

"Now faith is the substance of things hoped for, the evidence of things not seen."
Hebrews 11:1 (KJV)

As career advisors, one of our greatest challenges is to get clients to spend more time connecting with professionals rather than applying to actual jobs openings. To them, this is counter-intuitive. If they cannot see a job posting with an organization at this moment, they do not perceive the value in contacting someone who works there. They simply accept that the organization is not hiring. Their near-sightedness often results in missed opportunities and prolonged job searches since visible positions attract more competition. Tapping into the hidden job market to

Identify pending vacancies or positions that have not been created so far

is where Christian job seekers should have a particular advantage. Faith is forward-looking. It believes in that which has not yet materialized.

Conduct your job search by faith and not just by sight using direct marketing and cold-calling methods. These strategies are still highly effectual if done correctly. First, find news on your target organizations. A product launch, new client, or grant funding received are indicators that an organization may need to hire soon and great fodder for a conversation or opening paragraph in an inquiry letter. Next, get the details on the manager of the department or initiative for which you would like to work. Look on the organization's website, do a Google search, or call the organization's main line for the name, email address, and phone number of the right person. Given that you do not know each hiring manager's preferred method of contact, use a combination of email, postal mail, and a phone call. For example, begin with a phone call and then follow-up with mail or vice versa. Do not simply ask the manager if he or she is hiring. Start off the communication by showcasing your knowledge of the company, next highlight your relevant background, and then state your desire to contribute to his or her team.

Your primary goal of initiating contact is to secure a meeting to discuss how hiring you could benefit them. If an interview is not extended, secondary objectives are to learn about the hiring process within that company and names of similar organizations that may be hiring. Do not allow the lack of evidence of a job discourage you from believing there may be one.

Your Job Search Task:

Write and send an Opportunity Inquiry Letter to 10 organizations on your target list. See page 100 for an example.

VOLUNTEER

"Remember to do good and help each other. Gifts like this please God" Hebrews 13:6 (NLV)

Volunteer. Yes, that's right. Work for free. It may seem odd that we are asking you to help others when you might need help yourself, whether because you are feeling so depressed in your current job that it is hard to get up in the morning or you have been unemployed for some time already and can barely make ends meet. However, volunteering can actually positively affect your job search for several reasons.

First, we are wired in such a way that doing something meaningful, bringing joy and hope to others, and producing tangible results makes us feel good. When in a positive state of mind you will be able to job search with renewed energy and determination. Also, when you are keeping busy it is less likely that negative thoughts will have time to settle into your mind or worry you about when you are going to receive an application status update.

Second, volunteering allows you to

Continue operating in your gifts, talents, and expertise.

Employers are often reluctant to hire individuals with extended gaps in employment. Volunteering in a capacity or organization that is related to the type of work that you are seeking is a way to enhance your portfolio and make yourself more marketable. By looking at the United Way website, you might be surprised to discover the need for volunteer Communications and Marketing Managers, Art Teachers, Financial Counselors, Management Consultants, Licensed Barbers or Stylists, and Board of Directors Members. Experience is experience. On your résumé, volunteer positions should be treated just like paid positions. List the organization name, location, a title that communicates your contribution, dates, responsibilities, and accomplishments. In interviews, you should similarly feel comfortable highlighting the skills you honed and the impact you had in your volunteer role.

Third, volunteering allows you to get from behind your computer and connect with people. Remember, the more people who know who you are, what you can do, and that you are looking for a job, the better. Your volunteer position could directly or indirectly lead to a paid job.

Your Job Search Task:

Identify a place where you could be of professional service and arrange a volunteer commitment of 1-2 hours per week during your designated job search time.

PRACTICE INTERVIEWING

"Let no corrupting talk come out of your mouths, but only such as is good for building up, as fits the occasion, that it may give grace to those who hear." Ephesians 4:29 (ESV)

From our experience as career advisors, we know that job seekers often spend a lot more time refining their résumé than they do honing their interviewing skills. Remember, your application materials only get you to the interview phase. It is usually not until after a second or third round interview with multiple people in the organization that you may be extended a job offer.

Prospective employers generally use interviews to assess three factors: 1) Are you qualified to perform the functions of the position?; 2) Is your work ethic strong enough that you will consistently do a job well?; and 3) Do you fit with the people and culture of the organization? Said more simply, can you do the job, will you do the job and are you the type of person they would want to have working at their organization? You must have the correct words to articulate that you are the ideal choice. To avoid corrupting your chances of getting hired, you must

Speak confidently about your training, experience, and abilities

as they relate to the position. An interview is not the place to be self-deprecating. You must be constructive. If asked about a challenging situation you have encountered at work, talk positively about how you handled the issue and what you learned from it. An interview is not the forum to blame or complain about a former employer or colleague. You must communicate your thoughts cogently. Rambling and the use of fillers such as "umm," "like," and "you know" are extremely distracting to the listener and take away from your overall message. An interview is not the occasion to improvise. You should know whether what you have rehearsed in your head sounds just as good when it comes out of your mouth.

Practice is the key to interviewing successfully. However, do not use actual interviews with real employers as practice sessions. Before an employment interview, conduct a mock or practice interview with someone who will give you honest feedback. Career coaches, advisors, mentors, and professionals working in a related position are good choices.

Your Job Search Task:

Arrange and conduct a practice interview.

TELL YOUR STORY

"Then Jesus told them this parable: "'Suppose one of you has
a hundred sheep and loses one of them. Doesn't he leave the
ninety-nine in the open country and go after the lost sheep
until he finds it? And when he finds it, he joyfully puts it
on his shoulders and goes home.'" Luke 15:3-6 (NIV)

The Bible is full of parables. In fact, there are 46 parables told by Jesus that are recorded in the Gospels. Why might Jesus have chosen to use images such as the houses on rock and sand, weeds among good plants, lost sheep, a barren fig tree, and an invitation to a wedding banquet as a way to communicate his teachings? Perhaps, because He wanted His messages to be remembered.

Pictures are more likely to leave a lasting imprint on the brain than words alone. Therefore, in interview situations, you should make it your goal to paint pictures with your words. Do not just make claims about your knowledge, skills, and abilities, but rather,

Provide concrete cases to illustrate your points.

When asked questions like, how would you rate your analytical skills or what role do you tend to play on a team? Take the liberty of providing an example, even though one was not explicitly requested. Given that past behavior is a very good indicator of future behavior in a similar situation, interview questions that overtly ask you to share a story where you exhibited a particular quality are becoming increasingly popular.

A couple of common behavioral interview questions that solicit a vignette for a reply include "Tell me about a time when you had to work with a difficult team member" and "Share an experience where you had to work under strict deadlines." In such cases, structure your narrative in a way that is easy to follow by using the S.T.A.R. technique. Start with the **situation**, or the context. Next, briefly state the **task** or challenge that you faced. Then outline in detail the **action** steps you took to resolve the problem. This is where you present your qualifications for handling the responsibilities of the position at stake. Finally, wrap up your account with your **result**. This should either be your accomplishment or lesson learned. Specifics about the process you followed, tools you used, and quantifiable impact you had will make your story more vivid and credible. Make it easy for the employer to see why he or she should hire you.

Your Job Search Task:

Come up with illustrations from your academic or professional experiences that best exemplify your 3 greatest strengths.

MOVE ON

"but the people there did not welcome him, because he was heading for Jerusalem. When the disciples James and John saw this, they asked, "'Lord, do you want us to call fire down from heaven to destroy them?'" But Jesus turned and rebuked them, and they went to another village."
Luke 9:53-56 (NIV)

It is very uncommon, particularly in a tough job market, for a job seeker to obtain the first position to which he or she applies. This means you should brace yourself for the likelihood of being turned away not just once, but several times before a door is opened and you are welcomed in by a new employer. You will receive this NO in both direct and indirect ways. Most obviously, NO can come in the form of a rejection letter, email, or call from an employer; however, this professional courtesy is becoming increasingly rare. It is more likely that you will understand that you are no longer being considered for a position when you have not heard from the organization several weeks after submitting your application and you do not get a response to your follow-up communication to inquire about the status of your candidacy.

Fortunately, your employment future is not in the hands of the employers. How you react to being turned down is what will determine the course, length, and success of your job search. Like James and John, will you try to seek retaliation in your anger? This comeback could jeopardize your professional reputation. Will you wallow in self-pity and give up on the job search altogether? This response would mean that you remain stagnant in your current situation. Or, will you follow Jesus' example and simply move on to

Find opportunities elsewhere?

There is no doubt about it. It hurts to be denied something you believe you deserve, need, or want. When you come to understand that a certain position is no longer an option, take a moment to acknowledge your feelings of disappointment and frustration. But, only a moment! In order to keep up the momentum in your job search, you must take positive action quickly. If you are sincerely interested in working for an organization, consider responding to their rejection with a polite email or letter to the hiring manager to express your desire to be considered for future employment opportunities. A sample letter of this nature can be found on page 103. In any case, it will be extremely important for you to **redefine that N.O. (no offer) to N.O. (next one)** and keep applying to vacant jobs and talking with others to uncover pending positions. Think of getting a NO as a prompt for you to move on to the next one, and the next one, until the next one becomes the right one.

Your Job Search Task:

Apply for 3 more positions.

GET IN POSITION

"for an angel of the Lord went down at certain seasons into the pool, and troubled the water: whosoever then first after the troubling of the waters stepped in was made whole..."
John 5:4 (KJB)

When asked how they got to where they are, many working professionals will say that they secured their position by luck. They happened to strike up a conversation with someone at a birthday party which led to a job referral or they were volunteering at an organization just as a paid position became available and they were promoted into that role. As Christians, we know that pivotal events like this do not occur by chance, but as a result of God's hand on our lives. Does this mean that you should wait idly for God to move on your behalf? No. Although God could deliver a job to you while you are sitting on the couch watching TV and eating a bag of potato chips, it is unlikely.

From this scripture, we see that it is sensible for you as a job seeker to position yourself in the vicinity of locations known for restoring individuals to a healthy employment status. Obvious

"**P**ools" for you to frequent include career fairs, professional conferences, networking events, and job search clubs

where employment opportunities are readily shared. However, less obvious "pools" may include your hairdresser's chair, the coffee shop, or gym situated next to one of your target employers.

In essence, you must step out to put yourself in a place where there is an increased likelihood that you will hear news of upcoming changes within an organization or will meet someone who may know about a job. Better yet, why not go ahead and step in the water and wait for it to be "troubled." This way you will most definitely be the first one blessed with full employment! These more aggressive approaches include building relationships with employees within your target employers through conducting informational interviews or working in a part-time, seasonal, or internship position. Do not instantly discredit temporary jobs because of your credentials or years of experience. It is very common for such positions to be extended indefinitely or converted into full-time hires when organizations are "troubled" with the unexpected departure of an employee or a large project that requires more staff. Position yourself for a job search blessing.

Your Job Search Task:

Look for and apply for temporary jobs within your target organizations.

BE FLEXIBLE

"...Esther was also taken to the king's palace and entrusted to Hegai, who had charge of the harem. The girl pleased him and won his favor." Esther 2:8-9 (NIV)

Have you ever heard of the saying "man plans and God unplans?" How can this seemingly inconsistent statement be an important piece of wisdom for your job search? Queen Esther's story is an exemplary illustration of God rewarding someone being flexible and trusting of His plan for their life. The Bible does not say much about Esther's life before being captured by King Xerxes' men except that she was of Jewish descent, had no parents, and was raised by her Uncle Mordecai. Do you imagine her life's plan was to be kidnapped and placed in a harem? Most likely not. And, once she was put in this seemingly dreadful situation, God gave her several more uncomfortable and even dangerous challenges to overcome. She must have been terribly afraid and anxious as she entered the king's presence without his permission to do what she could to save the Jewish people. Esther's decisions to trust God and do what was right despite the circumstances and her feelings resulted in her preventing the loss of lives and becoming Queen Esther. What an awesome testimony she had!

In your employment search, we trust you are putting all of your efforts into finding the job you visualized earlier. It is a position which allows you to use your preferred strengths and skills to contribute to an organization in which you believe. This "planned-for" job might even be an opportunity to advance your career. While you are engaged in this search for the "perfect job" be mindful that like Esther,

God may have other plans for you.

He may need you in another place which may not be as desirable. Although you do not understand now, trust that God has a specific purpose for your life. He has not forgotten the desires of your heart. Keep Esther's experience and testimony in mind as you plan, pray, and obey God's calling on your job search.

Your Job Search Task:

Be open to unexpected opportunities.

TRY HUMILITY

"When he had finished washing their feet, he put on his
clothes and returned to his place."
John 13:12 (NIV)

You earned a degree or two in college. When people speak about you as a co-worker, "reliable, highly accomplished, and good guy" are the descriptors used. Yet, now that you are looking for a new job, it may seem unfair that you are regularly rejected for the type of positions you are highly trained and experienced in performing. And to further add to your frustration and anxiety, your savings account balance is getting lower and lower. You may be asking, Lord what does this mean? What should I do?

Look to also pursuing and, if offered, taking a "humble job" - one which would assist you in meeting your financial obligations and put you in an environment to be of service to God. Be assured there is no shame in doing work for which you are "overqualified."

Every job serves an important purpose,

necessitates know-how and dedication, even if a college degree is not required to do it. Our Lord, Jesus Christ, right before His betrayal and crucifixion, took on the job of washing the feet of His disciples. Christ was a leader and teacher who believed in modeling the behavior He wanted others to adopt. In answer to the question above "What should I do?" - is "What would Jesus do?"

Jesus would apply to any and all jobs that would give Him an opportunity to share the good news of God's grace, mercy, and love to others. Understand that there are many who will make disparaging remarks about you behind your back and in your face, and take great glee in seeing that you have nose-dived down the corporate ladder. Use these opportunities to explain to them that no matter your job title, you are always doing the good work of our Master. Should you take a modest position, it will not be your forever-one as you should continue to seek after your visualized job. For this temporary basis; however, you may find yourself getting closer to God by helping a co-worker in an area of your expertise or being a source of support while they are in distress. Philippians 2:4 supports this belief and reads "Each of you should look not only to your own interests, but also to the interests of others."

Your Job Search Task:

Apply to 3 jobs in which you could be of service to others.

STAND

"Therefore put on the full armor of God, so that when the day of evil comes, you may be able to stand your ground, and after you have done everything, to stand."
Ephesians 6:13 (NIV)

Given that there are so many things about the job search that are completely beyond your control---the economy, your age, nepotism, the mood of the person reviewing your application---it is certain that thoughts of self-doubt, fear, pity, and hopelessness will be sent by the evil one to come and attack your spirit and test your faith. How are you to remain committed to and hopeful, three months, six months, one year into your job search, when your spouse is wondering what you do all day or when you desperately want to earn the admiration of your children? You must

Draw inspiration from the truth that you are doing all you can within your realm of influence.

Keep doing what you are doing, and hold out for God to finish the battle for you.

The key to not giving up on your job search is tri-fold. First, you must honestly assess whether or not you are in fact doing *everything* you can to source employment opportunities and present yourself as the best candidate. You might discover that there is more that you can do like broadening your employment focus or geographic target, following-up on applications, conducting practice interviews, or spending

70

more time talking to people. Remember, having work to do will renew your sense of purpose and keep your mind busy so that it has less time to worry or think self-defeating thoughts. However, if you determine that you are truly doing all you can, you should draw peace from that reality.

Second, you must stand. To stand is not passive. It requires one to actively remain fixed in opposition to the forces that may try to sway them off course. To stand is to be stubborn. It is to be persistent in your job search efforts regardless of the circumstances. Keep looking even though you have not seen any opportunities posted in the last week. Keep networking even if it takes sending twenty-five informational interview requests to get a single reply. Keep applying despite the fact that others are getting laid off from their jobs.

Third, trust God at His word. "For I know the plans I have for you, declares the Lord. Plans to prosper you and not to harm you, plans to give you hope and a future" (Jeremiah 29:11).

Your Job Search Task:

Do not give up! Do any of the job search activities discussed in this book so far (again, if necessary).

SEEK HELP

"She said to herself, "'If I only touch his cloak, I will be healed.'" Matthew 9:21 (NIV)

In our society, we tend to admire people who can "hold it together" and "keep a stiff upper lip" when encountering trials and troubles. Looking for a job is arduous and thus tiring and the constant rejection and lack of feedback can be discouraging. In addition to the mental and emotional needs you might face during your job search, you may find yourself struggling with some of the job search tasks such as conducting informational interviews with strangers, writing an accomplishment-based résumé, and rewarding yourself.

What are some of the signs of needing help? Prolonged or overwhelming sadness, chronic fatigue, and social avoidance are symptoms which indicate that you may need support to better manage your thoughts and emotions. General confusion about why you have not been able to secure work, a lack of confidence in your ability to market your previous experience and skills, and a resistance to doing the assignments that have a higher probability of connecting you with others all signify that you would benefit from seeking job search assistance.

Support can come in various forms, such as self-help books or talking with friends and loved ones. If those resources do not provide you with tangible solutions,

Talk to a person trained to address your concerns.

If someone you know has seen a counselor or career coach, ask them for the person's name. Or begin with your pastor or family doctor. Once you have a few referrals, it is okay for you to inquire about their credentials, method of treatment, and any other items to determine if they are a good fit for you.

Certainly there are times when it is wise to keep our own counsel and others when it is foolhardy to go it alone. If you are thinking "I might need help," act on that thought. Receive it as the Holy Spirit whispering to you not to wait any longer. Go get the help you need.

Your Job Search Task:

Find a professional counselor or job search coach to assist you during this season.

REJUVENATE

"And He withdrew himself into the wilderness, and prayed."
Luke 5:16 (KJB)

As a job seeker, there are numerous competing priorities for your attention. We have given you Job Search Tasks on top of your regular responsibilities to your family, church, and current employer, and there are always unexpected demands like needing to console a friend in crisis. Before you begin to feel worn down by trying to respond to all of the calls on your life,

Prioritize time for self-care.

Even Jesus needed some time away from the masses and his disciples to rejuvenate himself. What might you do during your "me time?" Perhaps, spend a few minutes outdoors basking in the beauty of God's creation, relax the tension in your body and God's temple through yoga or a massage, or if you cannot go away on a prayer retreat, simply meditate on one of your favorite scriptures. Are there other kinds of activities that make you smile or give you a sense of fulfillment? Maybe gardening, hitting golf balls, or listening to good music? You might even decide to pick up a long lost hobby or take a class which taps into a new interest.

Another way to increase your energy and morale is to acknowledge your hard work and persistence in the job search. Take a few moments to reflect on all the Job Search Tasks you have completed, self-imposed deadlines you have met, and bold actions have taken. In order to remain in top mental, emotional, and physical condition to progress in your job search, you must take care of yourself.

Your Job Search Task:

Spend some time alone with God in prayer.

KEEP GOING

"Trust in the Lord with all your heart; do not depend on your own understanding. Seek his will in all you do, and he will show you which path to take." Proverbs 3:5-6 (NLT)

Did you ever go on road trips with your parents as a child? Do you remember asking the question "Are we there yet?" Your mother or father probably looked at you exasperatedly through the rear view mirror and said "Not yet" for the tenth time. The implied message was "Relax, I've got you covered, and you will know when we arrive."

Fast forward to today and you are anxious about the uncertainties of when you will get your new job.

Take comfort in knowing that you and
the Lord are traveling together

on your job search journey. God is your spiritual GPS - kindly encouraging you to turn left onto Patience Parkway, turn right onto Determination Drive, and to continue for a while on Believers Boulevard.

Stay with Him. Do not get angry or frustrated and decide to ignore the sacred navigational directions He's providing because they do not feel right or because you think you know a shortcut. Doing so will cause you to hear the "recalculating" voice of God telling you that by changing course you are adding more time to the trip.

In the same way you trusted your earthly parents to get you to your destination safely, extend the same confidence to God. Believe He is with you when you are contacting companies that do not have advertised jobs or when you are nervous about making follow-up phones calls to employers. At every detour, traffic jam, and bump in the road, Jesus is offering you encouragement and saying "Don't give up." Like the young child in the back seat of the family car, you may not know how close or far away you are from the intended destination. Nevertheless, trust you will get there.

Your Job Search Task:

Complete a task from the list on pages 104-107 this week that you have not done before.

ACT ANYWAY

"Be strong and courageous. Do not be afraid or terrified because of them, for the Lord your God goes with you; He will never leave you nor forsake you." Deuteronomy 31:6 (NIV)

What if I'm rejected again? What if I never find a job that interests me? What if they don't like me? What if...?

These are only a few of the common questions many job seekers find themselves asking. Have you had any of these concerns? What others could you add to the list? Unfortunately, the potential answers are often paralyzing. Paralysis is a result of fear.

Fear is the four letter word in a job search.

For the job seeker, fear is a constant companion. How do you minimize or get rid of fear?

Be bold. If you think your résumé is in the decline pile, do some detective work. Determine a person to contact and call even though it says "no phone calls please" on the job announcement. Briefly describe your qualifications and ask for an interview. If that employer does not value what you have to offer, ask for a recommendation and/or referral to another company. If you think you did poorly in the interview, be courageous and ask for another one. If you were runner-up for a job, contact members of the interview team and let them know you would like to be considered for future employment opportunities. If you think the odds are stacked against you, use that as a reason to be daring.

Believe these actions are risky? You are right. They are intelligent risks, however, not foolish ones. Also, do not confuse boldness with rudeness. In all actions, polite professionalism is expected.

Instead of fearing rejection, embrace it in a constructive way. Partner with other job seekers and have a contest to see who can get the most rejections in a day. Or make a list of the top ten job search tasks you are afraid of and give a reward to the person who overcomes the most in a week.

Still anxious about being bold? That's okay. Act anyway.

Your Job Search Task:

Decide to be faithful and not fearful. Identify a smart risk and take it.

NO EXCUSES

"He replied, "'The man they call Jesus made some mud and put it on my eyes. He told me to go to Siloam and wash. So I went and washed, and then I could see.'" John 9:11 (NIV)

"**I**'m not outgoing."

"I don't have time."

"I keep getting rejected."

"I don't know anybody."

"I can't apply for this job because I might get called in for another job."

"I'm too tired."

"I don't think I should be judged based on my appearance."

"Nobody is hiring. Why bother?"

These are just a few of the excuses job seekers use for not implementing recommended and proven job search methods. Can you claim any of these as your own? If so, make the decision today to be like the blind man in this scripture. It seems as if he did not procrastinate, come up with reasons why the mud would not work, or even question the stranger, Jesus, who unexpectedly came along and provided assistance. The blind man swiftly followed our Lord's instructions; he went and washed and was immediately rewarded.

Consider for a moment that the time you spend thinking of and

R eciting excuses may be delaying a
blessing to you or someone else.

How different would this story be if the blind man had said "I don't feel comfortable going to Siloam right now; maybe some other time?" Instead of a testimony of obedience and faith, the narrative would have been an example of missed opportunity and foolishness. The partnership between procrastination and justification has deferred and shut-down many great plans and promises. How do you want your job search story to end?

Your Job Search Task:

Eliminate your job search excuses.

EVALUATE THE OFFER

"Do not neglect your gift, which was given you through a prophetic message when the body of elders laid their hands on you." 1 Timothy 4:14 (NIV)

P raise you Father! Hallelujah! Glory to the highest! After applying to numerous jobs, attending many networking events, keeping your social media profile updated weekly, and dozens of other job search tasks, you have finally gotten the offer you have been actively waiting for. The employer has called you on the phone, emailed you, or perhaps told you in person. Your prayers have been answered and you are eager to finally complete the job search. Never mind a yellow caution light, we are putting a big red stop sign in front of you and strongly suggest you not give your answer immediately and

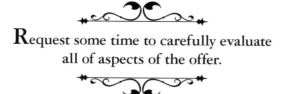

R equest some time to carefully evaluate
all of aspects of the offer.

Hopefully, you have been using the information from your visualized dream job to guide your job search. If not, pull it out now and create a "yes/ no" checklist to determine how the offered job compares to the visualized one. Here are some factors for you to consider. The correct answers are the ones which best suit you.

Salary - Does it represent at least what you need to pay your bills and save for rainy days? Does it reflect what your research has told you is the current value for someone with your experience in this industry and location?

Role expectations - You read the job posting and maybe got an explanation of the role during the interview. However, are you certain you understand what is expected of you? How the position fits into the overall framework of the organization? How your performance will be measured and rewarded?

Skill enhancement and development - Will this role be a repeat of what you have done previously or allow you to strengthen your knowledge, skills, and abilities in order to make you more marketable for your next job? Does the organization provide professional development training and promote service in professional organizations?

Values: Did you list flexibility, lots of teamwork, and a non-shared workplace as being important to you? Did you indicate a preference for being in a fast paced and high energy office? Do you value consistently getting work performance feedback?

Work team: What is the management style of your potential boss? Did you pick up any clues about what your co-workers would be like?

You may not know the answers to some of these questions. It is acceptable to call your future manger or human resources to ask. Assure them you are interested in making the best decision for everyone's benefit.

God wants us to be in a place where we can continue to utilize the key talents and gifts He's given us. Failure to do this at work may result in you feeling like you do not belong and lead to you being miserable. Most certainly it is important to look at all the aspects and determine if the good outweighs the bad.

Your Job Search Task:

Get the offer in writing. Create a list of the questions you need answers to and request a discussion with your potential supervisor. Ask God to tell you if this is where He wants you to be.

WRAP-UP RIGHT

"Oh, give thanks to the Lord! Call upon His name; Make known His deeds among the peoples!"
1 Chronicles 16:8 (NKJV)

You have accepted the organization's offer and have established your start date. You now have a new job! Hallelujah! You feel joy, excitement, relief, and ready to celebrate. In addition to thanking God and having your praise party, there are a few more career-related items to complete before this job search journey comes to an end.

Make thank you phone calls, or send emails, or notes to everyone who provided any form of assistance along the way (e.g., lifted you up in intercessory prayer, provided a target employer contact, conducted phone practice interviews, or consoled you during a bad day). Remind them of your

Offer to gladly be a resource

if ever needed.

Inform employers with whom you have applications under review that you are no longer available.

Update your LinkedIn profile to reflect your new employer, role, and responsibilities.

Prepare for this new opportunity by determining the constructive work habits you will bring and which unproductive approaches you will leave behind.

Your Career Management Task:

Build your reputation by appropriately communicating your new employment status.

CONCLUSION

"I know all the things you do, and I have opened a door for you that no one can close". Revelations 3:8 (NLT)

It is likely the job search journey you just concluded will not be your last. Because our God is one of change and growth, in 12 months, 5 years, or another time in the future, you may find yourself looking for a new position with your current employer or one that is not even in existence yet. While that thought may be a little unsetting, in Isaiah 41, God's word tell us 'Do not fear, for I am with you; Do not anxiously look about you, for I am your God. I will strengthen you, surely I will help you".

Here are suggestions you can follow that may make the next search easier.

Learn the rules: Meet with your manager during your first week to understand what success looks like to her (e.g., being on-time every day, speaking up in meetings, exceeding sales goals). Also read the company policy manual so you are clear on rules, such as personal use of your business email account and cell phone.

Be a record-keeper: Maintain an "accomplishment and contributions" log to keep track of how you have added value to the team. This will be extremely useful when writing résumés and preparing for interviews in the future.

Be engaged: Talk regularly and informally with co-workers to get updates on their work projects. Be alert to how you can assist them, and do it.

Be a life-long learner:

Learn new skills by attending company supported training programs, going to continuing education classes at the community college, or logging into webinars.

Continue networking: Get involved in a professional association which will allow you to connect with people from a variety of employers in the industry.

Be a helper: Share your job search advice and testimonies of God's goodness with others looking for employment.

EXERCISES AND EXAMPLES

Ideal job visualization exercise

Imagine you have secured a position that fulfills your passion and purpose. Write out your answers to the questions below. Paint the picture with words; be as descriptive as possible.

- What time of day is it as you get ready for work?

- What kind of clothes do you put on for work?

- How do you travel to work? How long does it take you to get there?

- What is the mission of your employer?

- In which city do you work?

- What is your work setting?

- What does your personal workspace look like?

- Are there other people working with you or near you? Who? What do they do?

- How do you begin your day?

- What kinds of projects do you tackle or responsibilities do you have?

- What knowledge and skills are you using that you really enjoy?

- How does your work support the organization?

- What about this work feels right and satisfying?

- Who do you connect with throughout your work day? How do you support them?

- What time does your work day end?

- What kind of quality of life does your job afford you?

My network diagram

You are surrounded by an extensive network of people who may be of assistance to you in your job search. Write down everyone who knows you by name in each of these categories. Share with them what kind of job you are seeking and ask them for recommendations of places to look or people to contact. Remember, networks are created. Strengthen your network by building relationships, particularly with industry experts and insiders at your target organizations.

Graduate school alumni	Industry Experts	Volunteer Work	Organization Insiders	Other
Parent's Friends	Mentor	Church	Hobbies/Clubs	Hairdresser/Barber
Extended Family	Immediate Family	**ME**	Close Friends	School Mates
Sorority/Fraternity	Sports Teammates	Colleagues	Neighbors	Children's School
Undergraduate School Alumni	LinkedIn Connections	Professional Association	Facebook Friends	Spouse's Friends

Form to help you tailor cover letters and résumés in response to a job announcement

Job title: _____

Organization name: _____

List all qualifications and responsibilities outlined in job announcement.	Place a check mark next to the qualifications and responsibilities you meet or have the potential to fulfill.	Demonstrate your ability to meet the qualifications and perform the duties. Provide a specific example for each using **STAR.** Situation or Task you faced, Actions you took, Results (positive) of your actions or lessons learned. Quantify outcomes whenever possible.

Note: The general rule of thumb is that you have at least 75% of the stated requirements to apply for a position. The next step is to incorporate this information into the cover letter and résumé you will submit for the job application. In your cover letter, highlight in detail your 2-3 strongest selling points. Incorporate all the ways you are qualified for the position in your résumé.

Information to gather on target organizations

When and where was the organization founded? Who were the founders?

What are the organization's purpose, mission, and values? What drives this company?

What is the work culture?

How is the company organized?

What are the short and long term goals? How can you influence those goals?

What new markets is the company considering? Or should it consider?

What are the major problems to be tackled?

How has this organization been successful in terms of products and services during the past year, five years, ten years?

Have there been recent cutbacks, layoffs, or restructuring?

What expansions, downsizing, or restructuring is planned?

Who are the members of the senior management team?

Does this organization need people to do what you are interested in doing?

Who are the staff members in the department you are targeting?

How could you complement the existing group?

How can you help meet the organization's objectives? What do you have to offer?

What is the organization's reputation?

What are the organization's strengths and weaknesses?

What organizations do employees tend to come from and move to next?

Who are the organization's competitors?

How is the organization impacted by public policies, global issues, etc.

What trends can you uncover in their sector?

Informational interview request (by referral)

Email Address: (always type last)
Email Subject: Monica Walker suggested I contact you

Dear Mr. Stroud,

I recently met Monica Walker at the American Association of Christian Counselors World Conference and she sends her greetings. Ms. Walker suggested I contact you, describing you as someone with valuable advice to give from your own experience working as a child, marriage, and family counselor.

This December I will complete a Master of Social Work degree from the George Warren Brown School of Social Work at Washington University in St. Louis. My goal is to obtain a position that will combine my experience and training in faith-based family counseling with my passion and determination to aid children in crisis situations.

Let me assure you Mr. Stroud, I do not expect you to have a job or know about a job. I only want your guidance. Would you allow me 30 minutes of your time sometime next week to discuss your insights and comments on pursuing such a career? I would greatly appreciate it. To more thoroughly introduce myself, I have attached my résumé.

Mr. Stroud, I hope that it will be possible for us to talk. If I do not hear from you within the week, I will telephone your office to inquire after a convenient time.

Sincerely,

Cynthia Simmons

Informational interview request (through research)

Email Subject: LinkedIn group member requests career advice

Dear Ms. Gigi Holmes,

We are both members of the Physical Therapists Network on LinkedIn and after reading your profile, I see that you are an expert in unconventional therapeutic practices which is an area of great interest to me. I am writing to request your advice and guidance on how to best transition into this specialty.

Would you allow me 25 minutes of your time next week to discuss your insights on pursuing this career? I would greatly appreciate it and assure you that I do not expect you to have or know about a job. To give you more detail on my background, I have attached a copy of my résumé.

Ms. Holmes, I hope it will be possible for us to talk soon and if I do not hear from you within a week, I will touch base with you again.

Best regards,

Mr. Tom Urban

Informational interview questions

In my research, I found that you have been in the _____field for over X years and received the "_____Award" last year. Would you share with me what you consider some of your other career highlights to be?

If you were looking for a job today what approach would you use?

What employers would be on your target list and why?

In your view, what is the employment outlook for this field?

How do you see the employment outlook positively and negatively impacting this company?

What is the future direction of this organization? What skills and experiences will be needed?

My research indicated company A, B, and C are your top competitors? In your opinion, is this accurate?

Why did you decide to work for this company?

What keeps you at this organization?

What impact do you believe _____(current or pending issue) will have on this industry?

Presently, what is the most critical challenge or problem impacting your team?

As you think about the skills and talents of your current team members, what competency or skill is missing? What would you add?

How does this department impact the rest of the company?

I have been an active member in the local chapter of the _____professional association for three years. What other organizations would you suggest I join?

When you interview candidates to join your team, what do you look for? What are your interview turnoffs?

After being interviewed, for what reasons are applicants usually not selected to work in your organization?

What process does your organization use to select interview candidates?

What 2-3 competencies/skills are most valued in this organization?

As you are aware, many organizations request salary expectations as part of the applicant screening process. In your opinion, what salary range do you believe is an appropriate expectation for someone with my background?

Would you please suggest other professionals I should contact for an informational interview? May I use your name as a reference in requesting the meetings?

After looking over my résumé, what suggestions do you have for how I can improve it?

If I have any further questions, may I contact you again?

Thank you for informational interview

Email Address: (always type last)
Email Subject: Thank you for informational interview on November 5

Dear Ms. Armstrong,

Thank you so much for taking time from your busy schedule to talk with me via phone on Tuesday. It was very helpful for me to learn so much about the current projects at the Smithsonian Institution and the career paths of several of your staff. I appreciate your suggestions on how I can make the most productive use of my job search time prior to being laid off. In fact, I have already signed up to take the online course in grant writing per your recommendation.

Based on what I learned from my talk with you and the research I have done, I am very interested in being considered for employment with the Smithsonian in the future. As a reminder, I have a strong background in administrative management, marketing, and development which would provide the Smithsonian flexibility to utilize me on various projects. I have enclosed a copy of my résumé to serve as a handy reference of my background, some of which I discussed with you when we spoke.

During the next few months I will stay in contact with you in hopes that there may be an opportunity to join your organization. Thank you again for your generous help, and I hope you enjoy a pleasant holiday.

Sincerely,

Peter Campbell

Reference page

References for Matthew John

Elizabeth Nicholas
Quality Control Manager
Houston Pharmaceuticals
2136 Fannin Street
Houston, Texas 77025
713.555.5555
enicholas@houstonpharm.com
Former manager

Joseph Whitfield
Processing and Production Director
Quaker Corporation
3017 H Street NW, Suite 411
Washington, DC 20005
202.555.5555 ext. 104
josephw3@quaker.com
Former manager

Constance Carey
Shipping and Receiving Associate
Quaker Corporation
3017 H Street NW, Suite 411
Washington, DC 20005
202.555.5555 ext. 107
constancec2@quaker.com
Former colleague

Opportunity inquiry letter

Dear Ms. Bynum,

I just read at ajc.com that Southern Company is evaluating expansion to the southwest. As a highly collaborative and strategically focused librarian, who has demonstrated value in providing solutions to my team members, I am writing to offer my experience to your company. Attached is my résumé, which will provide details on the career contributions I have made to my current and previous employers.

Highlights of my competencies include:

- Focused research skills using databases (Dialog, BIOSIS, and Lexis-Nexis)

- Strong bibliographic skills, including knowledge of MARC tags and LC headings

- Success resolving complex problems and managing special projects simultaneously

- Experience developing and providing training in both face-to-face and web-based instruction

I also have well-developed organizational and time management skills, work effectively on my own and in team situations, and have good conflict resolution abilities.

Ms. Bynum, I am confident there is a great deal I can contribute to Southern Company and would like to discuss with you the organization's upcoming needs. You can reach me at ydmaysx@ymail.com. If I do not hear from you in the next couple weeks, I will follow-up with you by phone.

Best regards,

Yvonne Mays

Follow-up after applying to job

Dear Pat Couch,

As a follow-up to the application I submitted for the C Developer position via Man Tech's online system last week, I would like to reiterate my interest in joining the Mission, Cyber and Intelligence Solutions Group. My eight years of experience in computer forensic analysis make me a great fit for the position. Additionally, I already have security clearance with the federal government.

For your convenience, I have attached my applications materials.

I look forward to the opportunity to learn more about your needs and further detail my qualifications during an interview.

Sincerely,

Kai Waters

Thank you for interview letter

Email subject: Team Lead Interview Follow-up

Dear Ms. Wang,

Thank you for the opportunity to interview for the Team Lead position yesterday.

I enjoyed learning more about Archstone's clients, new organizational structure and strategic priorities.

From our conversation, I understand your need for a collaborator, strategic thinker, and implementer. To the position, I would bring demonstrated success in building partnerships across a large organization, a systems-approach to addressing service delivery challenges, and commitment to increasing efficiency. I am confident I would make an effective leader during this time of transition at Archstone. Additionally, my supervisory style would capitalize on the strengths of the dedicated staff in place.

I appreciate your thoughtful consideration of my qualifications. Please feel free to email or call me if you need additional information, have any questions, or would like to offer me the job! Thank you for your time, and I look forward to hearing from you.

Sincerely,

Kevin Kutcher

Response to rejection letter

Dear Mrs. Russell,

Thank you for considering me for the Senior Engineer Project Manager position. I am pleased that you thought well enough of my qualifications to invite me for an interview and naturally disappointed in not being selected.

I appreciated the time that you and your team spent with me. Those meetings confirmed that Wheeler Manufacturing would be an exciting place to work to contribute to making household tools safer and more ergonomically-sound for your consumers. Please keep me in mind should another position become available. I would welcome the opportunity to talk with you again.

Best wishes to you and your fine staff.

Sincerely,

Jorge Sanchez

40 JOB SEARCH TASKS

1. Use O'Net - the Department of Labor website which provides free job information and career assessments.

2. Sign-up on Glassdoor - a free online career community to get inside information on jobs and companies.

3. If your city, county, or state offers job-specific training programs, attend and engage with the teachers. Find out about their background and share information on yours.

4. When attending any workshops, conferences, fairs, arrive early and stay late to provide organizers and presenters with event set-up or take-down assistance.

5. Join two different job search groups.

6. Register with a temporary employment agency.

7. Think of all the meetings (e.g., weight loss groups, knit & chat, prayer) and practices (e.g., swim, basketball, dance) you attend regularly. Take advantage of the opportunity for introductions and announcements to do your 30 second commercial and let the attendees know your employment interests.

8. Prepare a list of "ice-breaker" conversation starters through which you inquire about and share your passions or expertise with others.

9. Use your résumé to create and prepare for potential interview questions.

10. Gather information on one of your target employers. Seek answers to the following questions:
    a. Why does the organization exist (mission, how do they make money, etc.)
    b. What is the company's product line or service?
    c. Who are the company's competitors?
    d. What is the company's position relative to competitors?
    e. Where is the home office? Number of other offices and staff members?
    f. What are the company's current problems and potential opportunities?
    g. Who are the decision makers for the jobs you want?
    h. Who are the people you know at the organization?
    i. What does the employer need?

11. Identify the suppliers or contractors for your target employers and look for employment prospects with them.

12. Look through the contacts of those you are connected to on LinkedIn.

13. Get a part-time job.

14. Create a professional email signature block which includes your full name, email address, and phone number.

15. Get out of the house and spend time in public places 5 days a week.

16. Write out your script for an informational interview.

17. Practice saying your 30 second commercial every day to yourself, modifying it for various situations, such as a cook-out, church conference, elevator, family reunion, etc.

18. Join a public speaking group.

19. Research the activity of local and state economic development departments.

20. Read your college alumni magazine (including past issues) for leads on people to contact.

21. Read daily local and national newspapers and industry journals. Make note of the names and titles of people that interest you. Contact them to compliment and query them based on the article.

22. Wear apparel such as a college t-shirt or sports cap that is likely to spark a conversation.

23. Strike up a conversation with people at the airport, doctor's office, and other waiting areas.

24. Go to programs of interest at the local library and museum.

25. Do something you have never done before to place yourself amongst different people and expand your network.

26. Mail (not email) a letter of introduction and your résumé to a decision maker at your target organization. Request a meeting.

27. Post a recommendation for a LinkedIn contact.

28. Identify trade associations that are affiliated with the type of work you want to do.

29. Set up a career advisory board (4-6 people). Convene monthly meetings to discuss your job search plan and get advice.

30. Request practice interviews weekly with select networking contacts.

31. Make a list of people you know who are seeking work and help at least one person each week.

32. Write a 150-word biography to introduce yourself at a professional meeting.

33. Read an article on marketing and sales to get insights on how to market yourself.

34. Read an autobiography of someone you admire.

35. Develop a presentation on your areas of expertise. Share it with others by posting it on your LinkedIn page.

36. Find out where the employees of your target organizations have lunch. Eat there once a week.

37. Conduct a self evaluation:
    a. What are your five most important career accomplishments and how did you achieve them?
    b. How would your classmates and/or colleagues describe you?
    c. What interests you the most about the top 10 organizations on your target employer list?
    d. What were the positives and negatives of your last job?

38. Call, email, or write a letter to a person you have not spoken with recently to find out how they are doing.

39. Sign-up for RSS feeds on target employers.

40. Follow the news and the money. What "stimulus" measures are being implemented in your community? Begin developing relationships with employers which could be positively impacted by that pipeline.

SAMPLE JOB ANNOUNCEMENT WITH TAILORED RÉSUMÉ AND CUSTOMIZED COVER LETTER

UNIVERSITY CONFERENCE COORDINATOR

JOB ANNOUNCEMENT CODE: 1105566

MADISON (AREA 13)

LOCATION: Madison, WI

HIRING ORGANIZATION: The University of Wisconsin-Madison, Wisconsin Union Central Reservations Center serves the UW-Madison campus community and union members by planning and supporting educational, social, and cultural events campus-wide.

JOB DUTIES: Function as an event and conference planner for the Wisconsin Union; coordinate facilities usage for meetings, receptions, seminars and special campus events (10 to 500 participants); meet with clients to assess special equipment and set-up needs; develop event budget, services contracts, activity plans, and marketing campaigns; interpret and administer campus facilities policies and procedures; schedule space and set-up for events; and develop food and beverage service operations.

KNOWLEDGE REQUIRED: Excellent oral and written communication skills; public relations, customer service skills and problem solving skills; organizational skills; multi-tasking skills; knowledge of computerized reservations and/or scheduling systems and diagram software; conference services and meeting planning techniques and practices; catering and other food and beverage event planning and sales; desktop computers utilizing standard business hardware and software, e.g. database, word processing; electronic mail, and the internet; effective sales practices and systems; ability to work under pressure and handle multiple tasks simultaneously while receiving continual interruptions; quality negotiation skills to assist customers and service department providers; ability to work independently while maintaining excellent communication and internal/external relationships; communicate courteously, following customer service standards, to vendors, customers, and coworkers, often under stressful circumstances. The work must be performed within time constraints, meeting delivery schedules and internal deadlines.

Employment will require a criminal background check.

HOW TO APPLY: Download special application materials from the following web site: http://www.ohr.wisc.edu/COB/UNIVCONFCOORD_1105566.doc. If you would like the materials mailed to you, please contact Wisconsin Union, Human Resources Office at 608-263-3939.

DEADLINE DATE: Submit a letter of interest, current résumé and special application/examination materials by **Friday, January 13, 20XX**. Please submit application materials and a résumé to: Julie Medenwaldt, UW-Madison, Wisconsin Union, 800 Langdon Street, Madison, WI 53706 or email medenwaldt@wisc.edu. Application materials will be reviewed and the most qualified candidates will be invited to participate in the next step of the selection process.

Master résumé

Saskia N. Clay-Rooks

011 Glenallen Lane   Durham, NC 27708   919.207.37XX   saskia.clay-rooks@mail.com

PROFESSIONAL EXPERIENCE

Academic Advising Center, Trinity College of Arts & Sciences, Duke University, Durham, NC
Academic Advisor, August 2010-present

- Engage cohort of undeclared freshmen/sophomores in the processes of self-assessment and reflection necessary for devising coherent academic plans consistent with his/her life goals
- Approve course selections and clear students for registration each semester
- Foster students' development of strong navigational, strategic risk-taking and self-advocacy skills
- Monitor students' academic progress and integration into college life, recommending resources or making referrals as appropriate

Office of Career Services, Nicholas School of the Environment, Duke University, Durham, NC
Senior Career Specialist, August 2009-present

- Facilitate self-assessment/career exploration activities and present customized, tiered workshops to address professional development needs of students with varying levels of experience
- Provide advice to students through individual advising sessions on résumés, cover letters, networking, interviewing and job/internship search strategies
- Implemented strategic "just in time" model to increase first-year student use of advising services by 86%
- Oversee student engagement in university-wide internship program, including advertising opportunities, evaluating application/interview process and confirming placements of approximately 125 interns

- Coordinate on-campus recruiting visits for employers
- Responsible for weekly email digest to promote office events and employment opportunities
- Explore and implement use of interactive Web 2.0 technologies to deliver career services to students
- Served on planning committee for first-ever conference for all career services professionals at Duke
- Honored by student body with Staff of the Year Award during first year in position

Institute for Shipboard Education, Semester at Sea, Various locations
Living Learning Coordinator, Career Development, June-August 2011
- Traveled with 700 college students and lifelong learners to 7 countries in Europe and Northern Africa
- Assisted students in identifying and articulating how their international experience provided greater career focus and marketable skill enhancement
- Responsible for ship-wide activities and support for students in assigned residential area
- Enforced community policies and served as part of "on-call" response team while in port

College Summit,Various locations
Writing Coach Coordinator, July 2010
- Worked collaboratively as part of Core Staff team to ensure overall success of 4-day residential college preparatory workshops for rising high school seniors from low-income communities
- Trained 9-11 volunteer Writing Coaches from varying backgrounds on College Summit Writing Methodology for assisting students with producing college application personal statements
- Encouraged, monitored and troubleshot to ensure that Writing Coaches effectively implemented curriculum
- Served in role of Writing /College Coach 2007, 2008

University Career Services, University of Virginia, Charlottesville, VA
Assistant Director, Career Outreach Services, July 2006-July 2009
- Counseled diverse group of University students navigating career exploration, internship/job search and graduate school application processes
- Critiqued C.V.s/résumés/cover letters, conducted mock interviews and prepared students for contact with potential employers during career fairs/networking events
- Served as primary resource for underrepresented student populations, coordinating and expanding programs to meet their career-related needs by nurturing key relationships with student organizations, alumni, employers and other University offices
- Received National Association of Colleges and Employers (NACE) **Innovation Excellence Award** for designing and executing Multicultural Professional Development Conference
- Developed and coordinated career peer educator program, including goal setting and evaluation
- Trained and supervised 1 full-time staff member, 1 graduate assistant and 7-9 undergraduate student volunteers
- Successfully chaired search to fill 2 career counselor positions
- Reviewed applications and selected recipients as member of 2008 public service Internship Grant Committee

Graduate Assistant, Jefferson Extern Program, August 2005-May 2006
- Promoted extern (job shadowing) program to University students through small group orientation sessions and individual appointments
- Developed new partnerships with employers, confirmed extern assignments and reviewed student/sponsor evaluations
- Created externship manual for students

Learning and Interacting in Our Community, University of Virginia,
Charlottesville, VA
Facilitator, January-May 2006
- Guided weekly dialogue/activities for 35 first-year students to promote awareness and foster self-exploration of issues pertaining to race, class, gender and sexual orientation
- Led discussion for group of 10 students during breakout sessions; reviewed and responded to reflection papers and assignments online
- Conferred with co-facilitators and professor weekly to identify ways to enhance class discussion/ simulations and the overall design/ implementation of the program in its pilot year

Office of Undergraduate Admission, The College of William and Mary,
Williamsburg, VA
Assistant Dean, Multicultural Recruitment, June 2002-July 2005
- Planned and implemented recruitment and yield events including workshops, receptions, programs targeting multicultural students and a campus-wide program for all admitted students and their families as a member of the Programming Committee
- Advised the Multicultural Ambassador Council, a diverse 40 member volunteer student group, and co-supervised 3 student interns who supported multicultural outreach efforts
- Conducted one-on-one as well as group information sessions for up to 300 prospective students and their families
- Acted as primary reader and evaluator of approximately 1,250 applications, including international applicants, and served on the Admission Committee
- Evaluated applicants and made recommendations for full in-state tuition scholarship and summer bridge program
- Represented institution to college bound students at high school visits and college fairs during approximately 5 weeks of recruitment travel per year

EDUCATION

University of Virginia
Charlottesville, VA
Master of Education, Social Foundations, May 2006

The College of William and Mary
Williamsburg, VA
Bachelor of Arts, Black Studies, May 2002
Phi Beta Kappa

QUALIFICATIONS

Certified Federal Career Counselor/Job Search Trainer, April 2011
Myers-Briggs Type Indicator and Strong Interest Inventory Qualified
Interpreter, December 2006

VOLUNTEER SERVICE

Dress for Success, Career and Image Coach
College Summit, Writing Coach

PROFESSIONAL MEMBERSHIP

National Association of Colleges and Employers

Résumé tailored to job announcement

Saskia N. Clay-Rooks

011 Glenallen Lane   Durham, NC 27708   919.207.37XX   saskia.clay-rooks@mail.com

RELEVANT EXPERIENCE

Nicholas School of the Environment Office of Career Services, Duke University, Durham, NC
Senior Career Specialist, August 2009-present
- Coordinate on-campus recruiting visits for employers: assess needs, schedule dates, reserve rooms utilizing scheduling system, secure A/V equipment and set-up for events
- Served on planning committee for "One Duke" conference: determined agenda, worked within limited budget, developed menu and scheduled catering deliveries, negotiated service contracts and speaker fees
- Developed strategic "just in time" marketing campaign which increased first-year student use of advising services by 86%
- Responsible for weekly email digest to promote events
- Honored by student body with Staff of the Year Award in 2010

Institute for Shipboard Education, Semester at Sea, Various locations
Living Learning Coordinator, June-August 2011
- On team responsible for ship-wide community-building activities (up to 700 participants) such as orientation and Talent Show as part of an aggressive event schedule
- Adhered to and enforced strict policies to ensure safety of all on board

University Career Services, University of Virginia, Charlottesville, VA
Assistant Director, Career Outreach Services, July 2006-July 2009
- Received **Innovation Excellence Award** from National Association of Colleges and Employers (NACE) for designing and executing Multicultural Professional Development Conference: independently secured event sponsors, 35 presenters/panelists, conference center, food and beverage service

- Nurtured key relationships with student organizations, alumni, employers and other University offices to increase use of office services and seminar attendance by target constituencies
- Trained and supervised 1 full-time staff member, 1 graduate assistant and 7-9 undergraduate student volunteers

Office of Undergraduate Admission, The College of William and Mary, Williamsburg, VA
Assistant Dean, June 2002-July 2005
- Planned and implemented recruitment and yield events including workshops, receptions, banquets and overnight campus visits: coordinated transportation logistics, hosts, entertainment
- Played integral role in preparation for a day-long, campus-wide event for all admitted students and their families (up to 2,000 participants):
- Conducted one-on-one as well as group information sessions for up to 300 prospective students and their families
- Represented institution to college bound students at high school visits and college fairs

EDUCATION
Master of Education, Social Foundations, May 2006, **University of Virginia,** Charlottesville, VA

Cover letter customized to job announcement

Saskia N. Clay-Rooks

011 Glenallen Lane   Durham, NC 27708   919.207.37XX   saskia.clay-rooks@mail.com

January 13, 20XX

Julie Medenwaldt
University of Wisconsin -Madison
Wisconsin Union
800 Langon St.
Madison, WI 53706

Dear Ms. Julie Medenwaldt,

Whether through humor, shocking images, incredible movement or inspiring words there are certain events that have the power to create memories that last a lifetime. It is for this reason that I am thrilled to apply to be your next University Conference Coordinator (1105566). I have listed my qualifications which I am confident would enable me to make an immediate contribution as a member of the Campus Event Services team:

*10 years experience working on college/university campuses

*Familiarity with interpreting and administering campus policies and procedures

*Coordinated events ranging from one-hour meetings for 10 participants up to day-long campus-wide special events for up to 2,000 participants

*Proven success having received national recognition for conference I planned

*Received staff of the year award for providing excellent customer service

*Public relations experience as first point of contact for various university constituencies

In the numerous university positions have I held, the most enjoyable and rewarding of my responsibilities have included seeing an event through from concept to execution. I am motivated by the prospect of being able to use my communication skills, organizational talents, and conference and meeting planning experience to serve the UW-Madison community by arranging and supporting educational, social, and cultural events campus-wide. Given the recent opening of New Union South, renovation of Memorial Union, and number of events, particularly those that are free and open to the public, I know it is an exciting time to be at UW-Madison.

My résumé is attached for your review and I would welcome the opportunity to further discuss my qualifications for the position during an interview. Thank you for your thoughtful consideration.

Sincerely,

Saskia N. Clay-Rooks

ABOUT THE AUTHORS

Saskia N. Clay-Rooks and Glenda Sullivan Lee, SPHR are experienced Christian career development professionals. Clay-Rooks has worked in career services at several premier universities and Lee has held recruiting, interviewing, and hiring responsibilities at fortune 100 companies in addition to 10 years in higher education. With a combined total of over 35 years of experience, they have helped thousands of job seekers successfully secure meaningful work consistent with their purpose, values, and talents.

Made in the USA
San Bernardino, CA
09 July 2014

13116576R00074